My Phonics Book

UPPER-CASE

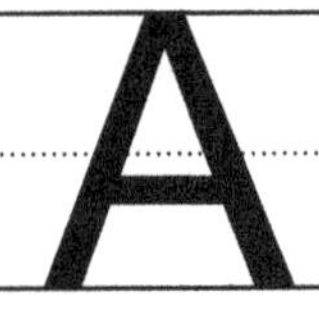

lower-case

a

These pictures begin with the letter A,a. Color the pictures.

UPPER-CASE

B

lower-case

b

These pictures begin with the letter B,b. Color the pictures.

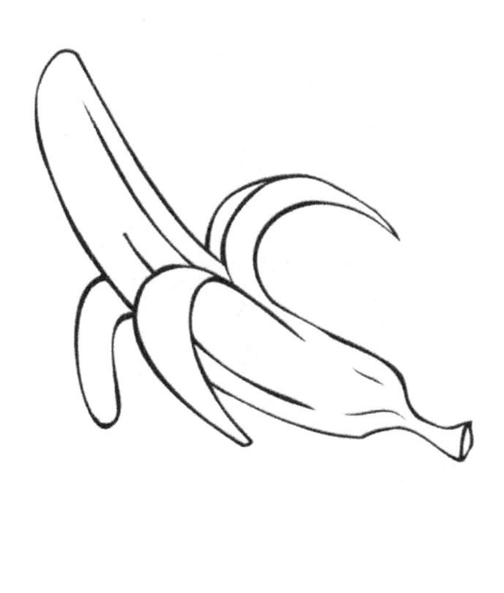

UPPER-CASE

C

lower-case

c

These pictures begin with the letter C,c. Color the pictures.

UPPER-CASE

D

lower-case

d

These pictures begin with the letter D,d. Color the pictures.

UPPER-CASE

E

lower-case

e

These pictures begin with the letter E,e. Color the pictures.

These pictures begin with the letter F,f. Color the pictures.

UPPER-CASE

G

lower-case

g

These pictures begin with the letter G,g. Color the pictures.

UPPER-CASE

H

lower-case

h

These pictures begin with the letter H,h. Color the pictures.

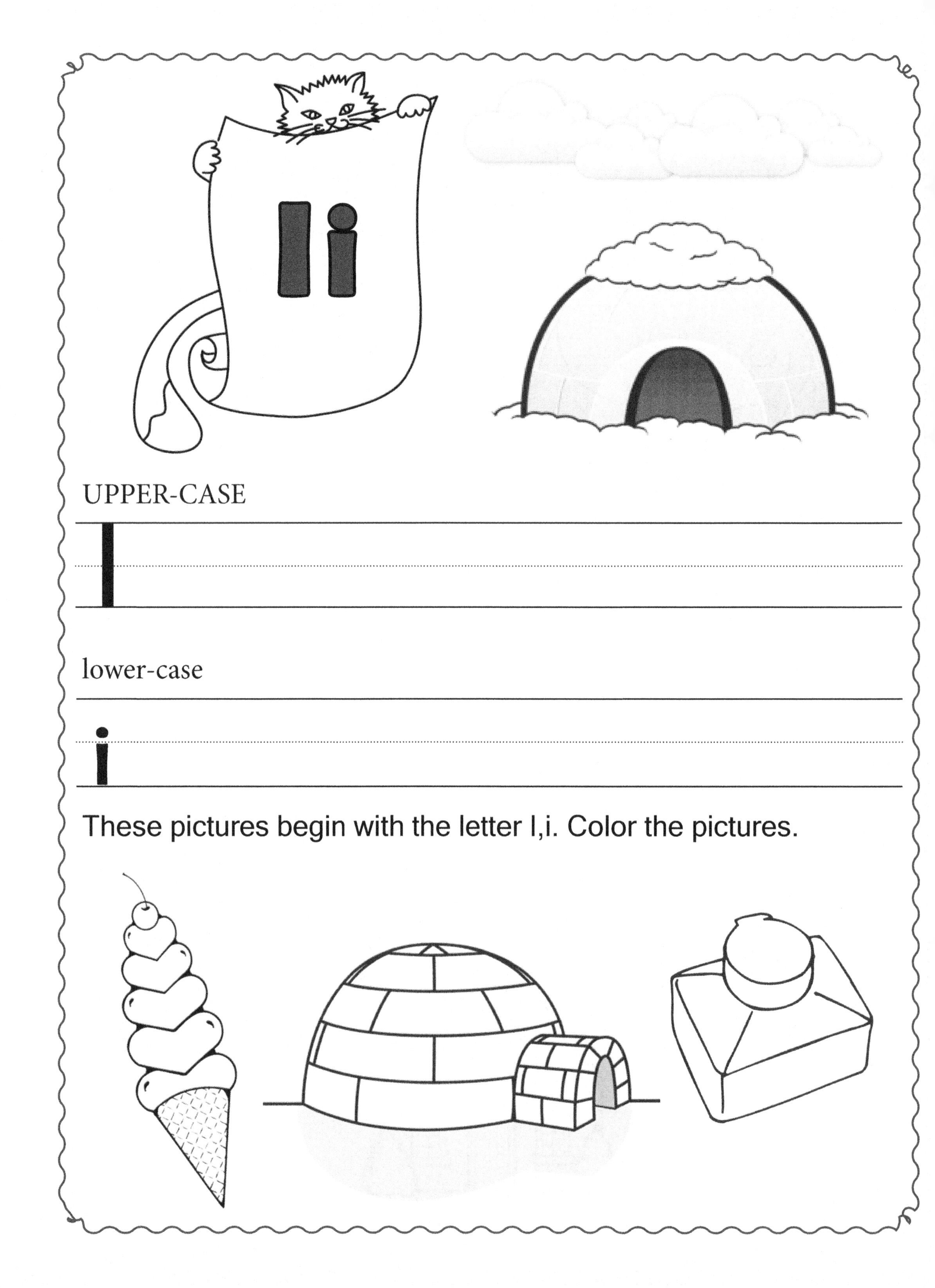

Ii
UPPER-CASE
I
lower-case
i
These pictures begin with the letter I,i. Color the pictures.

Jj
UPPER-CASE
J
lower-case
j
These pictures begin with the letter J,j. Color the pictures.

UPPER-CASE

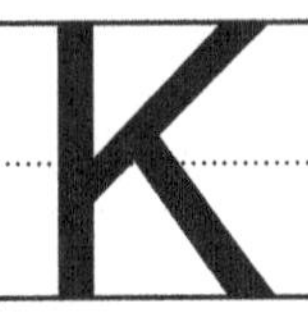

lower-case

These pictures begin with the letter K,k. Color the pictures.

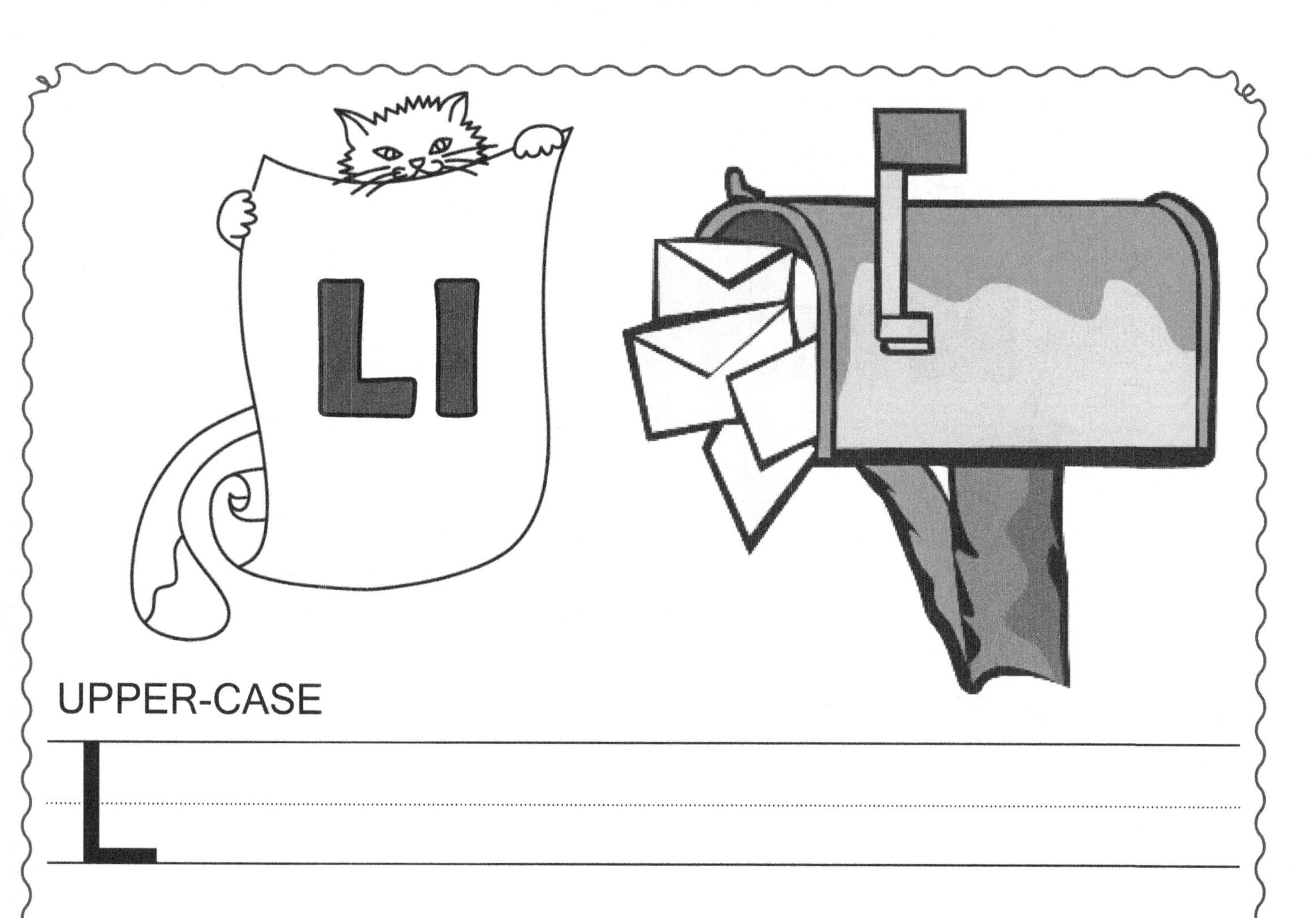

UPPER-CASE

L

lower-case

l

These pictures begin with the letter L,l. Color the pictures.

UPPER-CASE

M

lower-case

m

These pictures begin with the letter M,m. Color the pictures.

UPPER-CASE

N

lower-case

n

These pictures begin with the letter N,n. Color the pictures.

UPPER-CASE

O

lower-case

o

These pictures begin with the letter O,o. Color the pictures.

UPPER-CASE

P

lower-case

p

These pictures begin with the letter P,p. Color the pictures.

UPPER-CASE

lower-case

q

These pictures begin with the letter Q,q. Color the pictures.

UPPER-CASE

R

lower-case

These pictures begin with the letter R,r. Color the pictures.

UPPER-CASE

S

lower-case

s

These pictures begin with the letter S,s. Color the pictures.

Tt
UPPER-CASE
T
lower-case
t
These pictures begin with the letter T,t. Color the pictures.

UPPER-CASE

lower-case

These pictures begin with the letter U,u. Color the pictures.

UPPER-CASE

lower-case

These pictures begin with the letter V,v. Color the pictures.

UPPER-CASE

W

lower-case

w

These pictures begin with the letter W,w. Color the pictures.

Xx
UPPER-CASE
X
lower-case
x
These pictures begin with the letter X,x. Color the pictures.
TOOTH

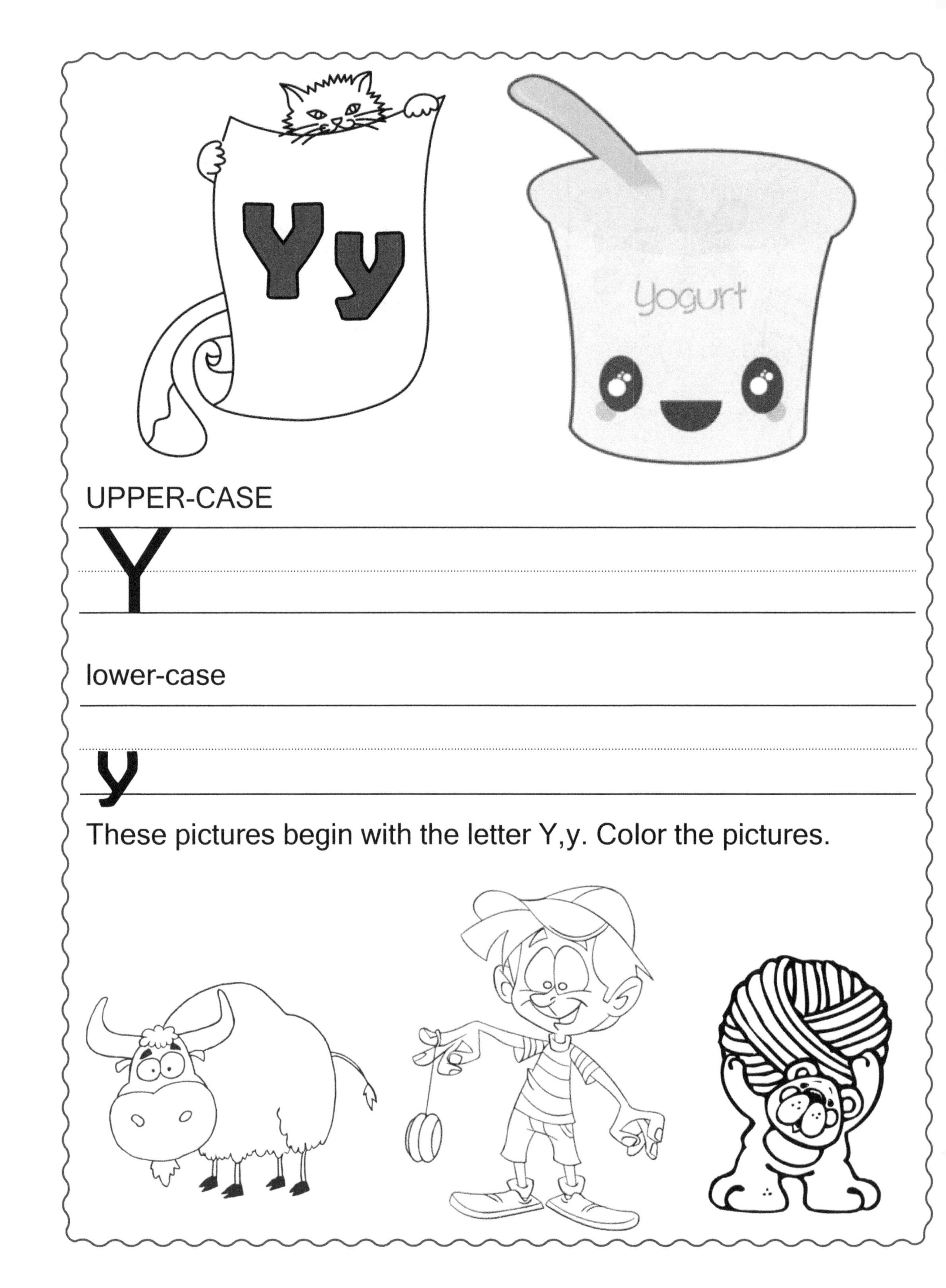

Yy
Yogurt
UPPER-CASE
Y
lower-case
y
These pictures begin with the letter Y,y. Color the pictures.

UPPER-CASE

Z

lower-case

z

These pictures begin with the letter Z,z. Color the pictures.

Name...................................

Phonics Beginning Sounds

____at

____at

____at

____at

____at

____at

____at

WORD LIST

s b f

h r c m

Name.......................................

Phonics Beginning Sounds

____ an

____ an

____ an

____ an

____ an

____ an

____ an

WORD LIST

m f r

v c t p

Name.....................................

Phonics Beginning Sounds

____en

____ag

____ed

____am

____ake

____ead

____un

WORD LIST

fl s c

cl br t b

Name..................................

Phonics Beginning Sounds

___og

___all

___oose

___gg

___ish

___ar

___ape

WORD LIST

b f e

gr c g d

Name..................................

Phonics Beginning Sounds

ug

ick

orn

oll

eet

oat

WORD LIST

h g c

f d ch b

Name.......................................

Phonics Beginning Sounds

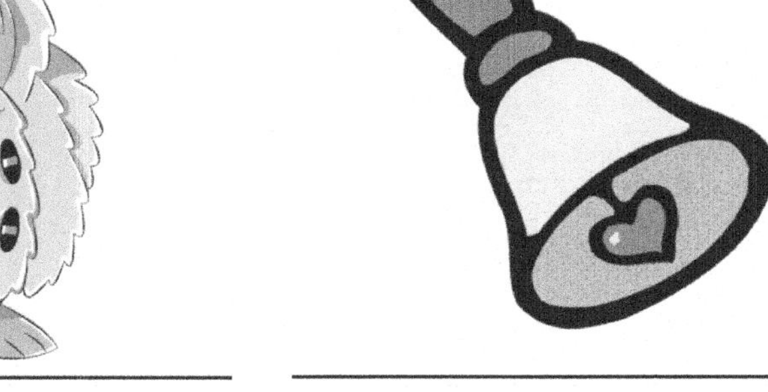

____oat ____ell ____ab

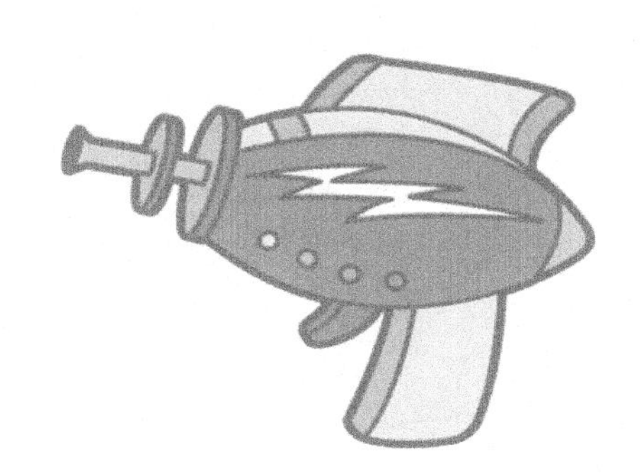

____ox ____un ____ome

____am

WORD LIST

j h cr

f c g d

Name..............................

Phonics Beginning Sounds

___ox

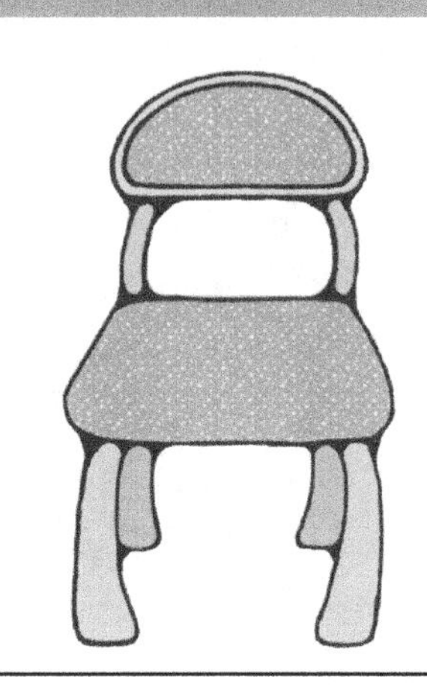

___air

___ish

___og

___um

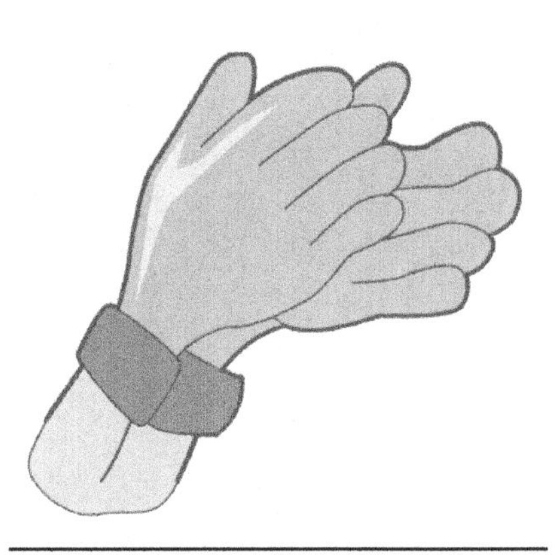

___and

___ug

WORD LIST

h c d

g j b fr

Name..................................

Phonics Beginning Sounds

____ee

____ow

____um

____ouse

____et

____id

____eg

WORD LIST

j b h

k l dr cr

Name……………………………

Phonics Ending Sounds

k_____

b_____

p_____

f_____

w_____

b_____

s_____

n_____

Name.................................

Phonics Ending Sounds

s______

c______

m_____

l______

c______

b______

b______

m_____

Name....................................

Phonics Ending Sounds

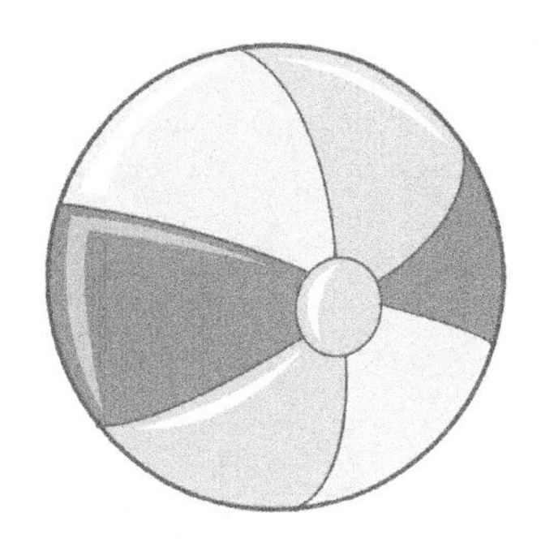

b_____

g_____

b_____

gl_____

cl_____

h_____

c_____

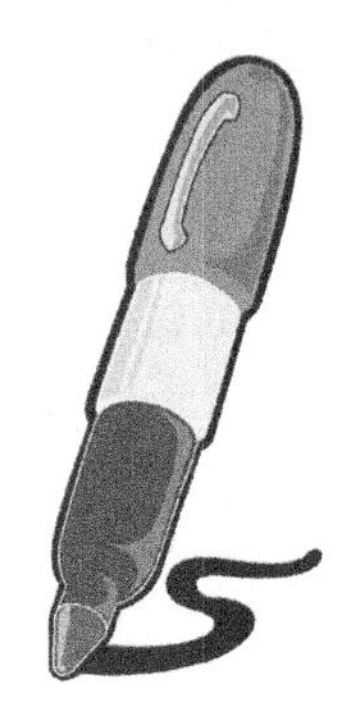

p_____

Name.....................................

Phonics Ending Sounds

n______

b______

p______

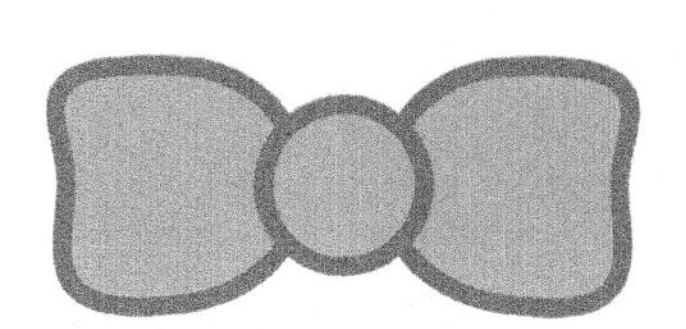

b______

b______

m______

w______

c______

Name.................................

Phonics Ending Sounds

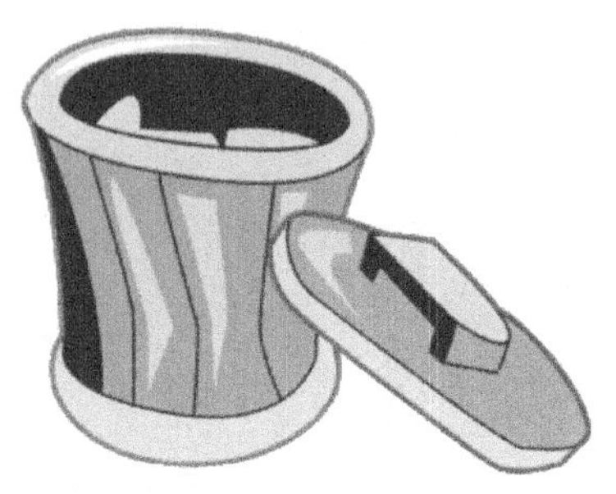

l_____

m_____

m_____

n_____

m_____

n_____

r_____

n_____

Name...................................

Phonics Ending Sounds

p_____

sn_____

h_____

sn_____

p_____

n_____

r_____

n_____

Name.................................

Phonics Ending Sounds

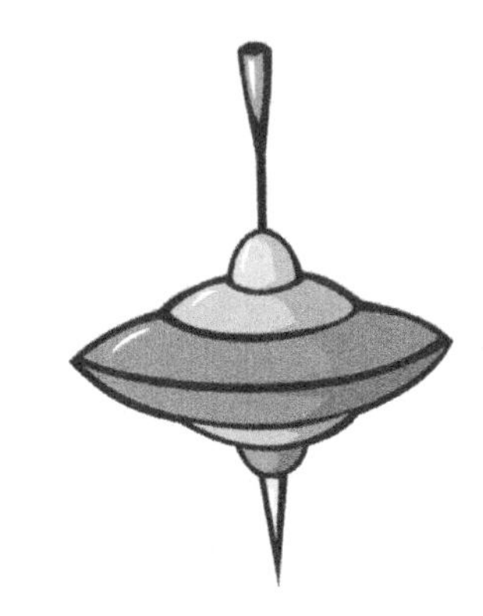

t_____

y______

t_____

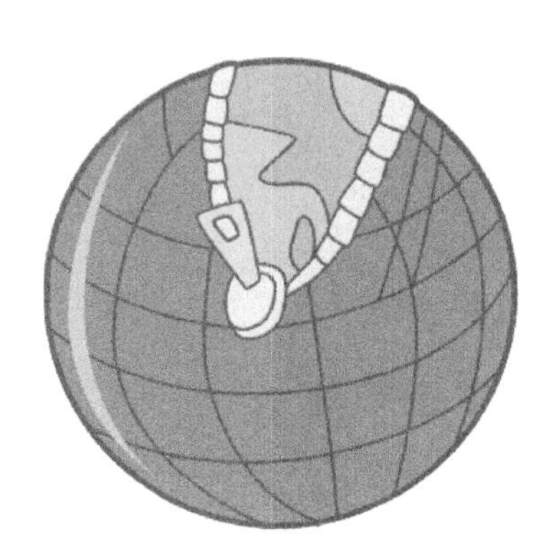

z______

v______

t______

v______

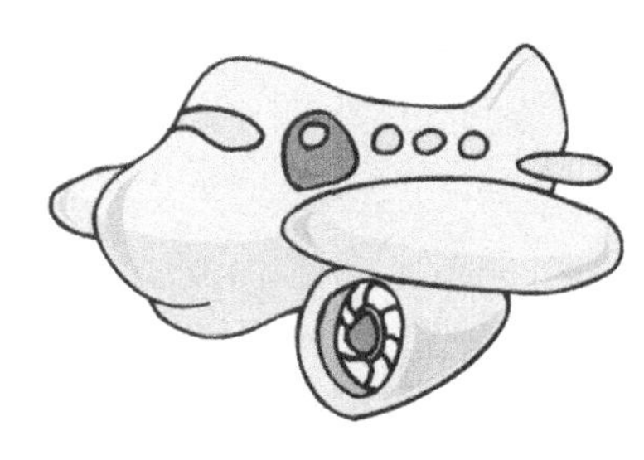

pl_____

Name..................................

Phonics Ending Sounds

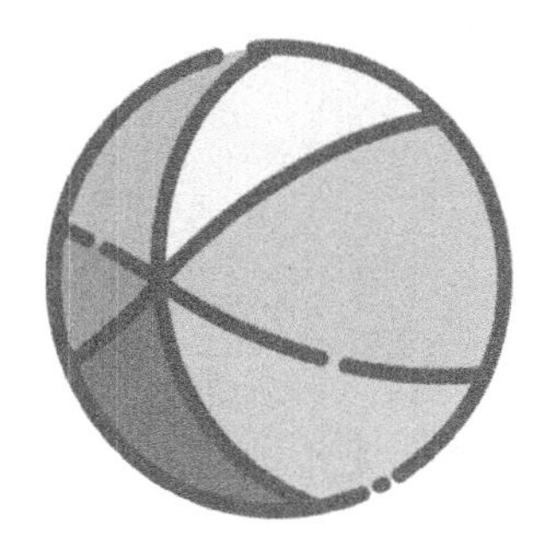

b______

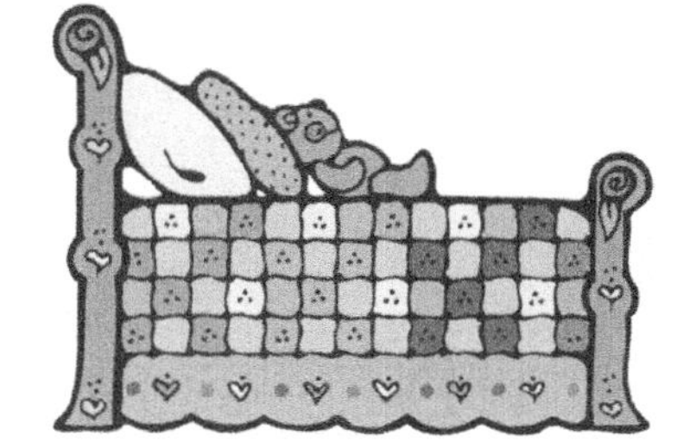

b______

b______

c______

c______

d______

d______

b______

Name.................................

Phonics Ending Sounds

b______

c______

b______

c______

cr______

d______

fl______

b______

Name.....................................

Read, Circle and Write

bee we

mat bat

back sack

bed fed

tin bin

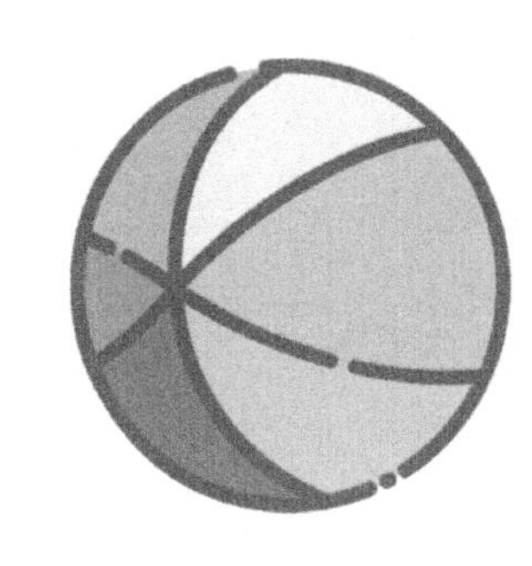

hall ball

mug bug

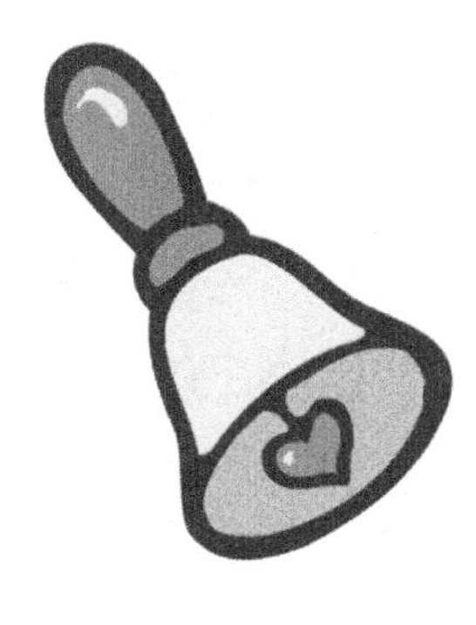

bell tell

bake cake

Name...................................

Read, Circle and Write

ben ten

boat goat

fox  box

hit pit

jar car

fat cat

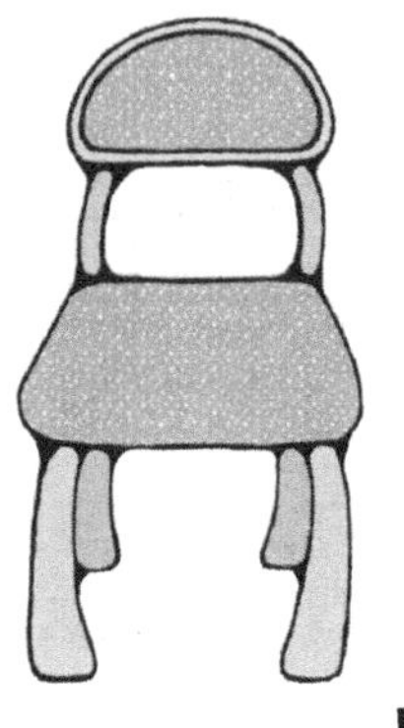

chair hair

brick chick

clam jam

Name.................................

Read, Circle and Write

grab crab

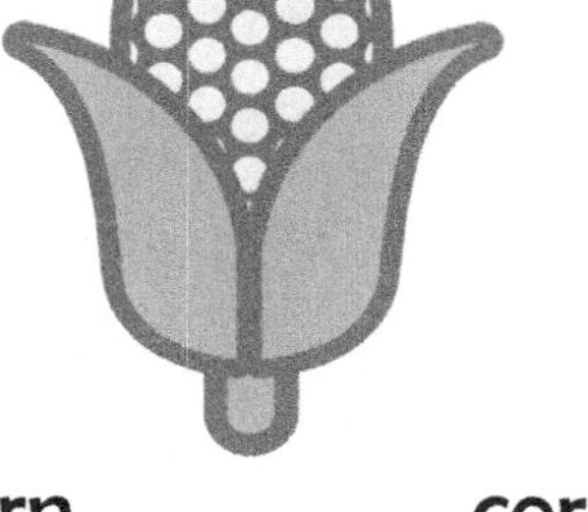

born corn

crow low

deer beer

dog fog

tall doll

luck duck

eight weight

book look

Name..................................

Read, Circle and Write

ban fan

fat bat

feet sheet

hire fire

fish dish

slag flag

fox box

frog jog

girl twirl

Name.................................

Read, Circle and Write

boat goat

goose moose

grape crape

care bear

sum gum

gun fun

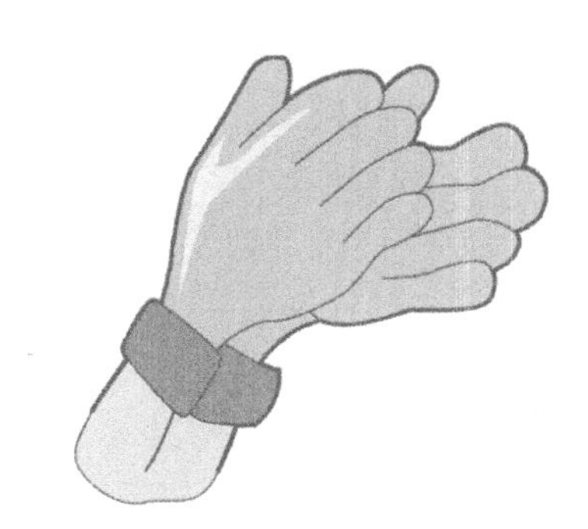

hand land

bread head

hen pen

Name.....................................

Read, Circle and Write

ram jam

horse force

home dome

dam jam

jug hug

jump dump

kid bid

ping king

beef leaf

Name.................................

Read, Circle and Write

bag drag

cap nap

rat bat

pup cup

rat hat

mad had

clap map

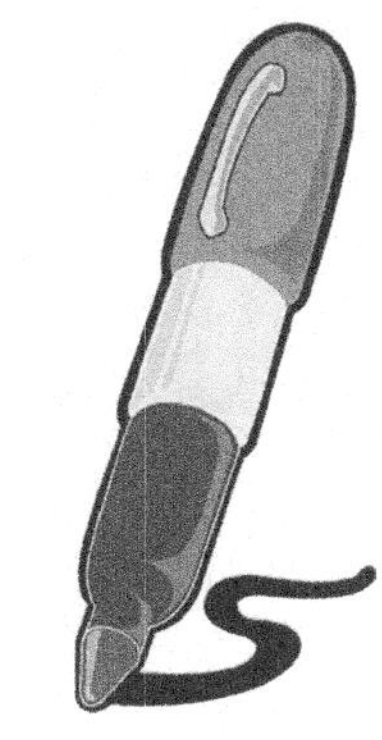

hen pen

herd bird

Name................................

Read, Circle and Write

cake bake

lock clock

bed sled

fall mall

hem jem

glass class

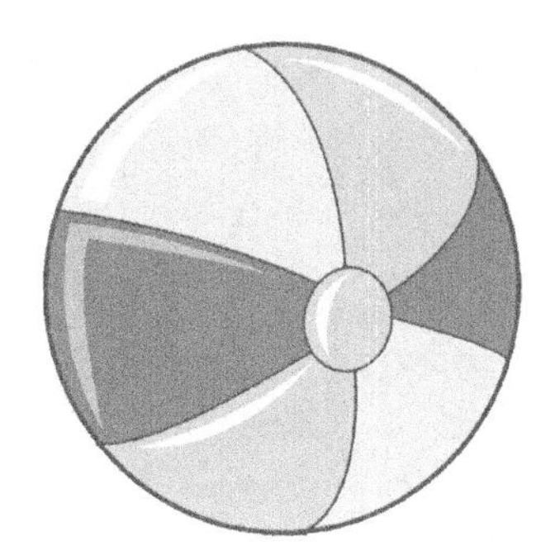

call ball

lock dock

bike pike

Name....................................

Read, Circle and Write

mug jug

yard card

pipe ripe

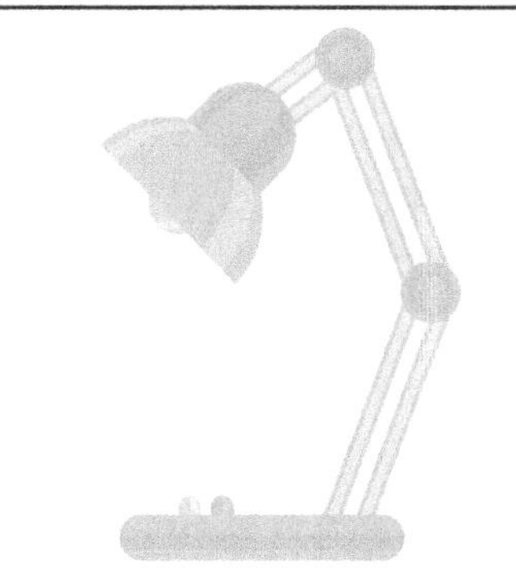

camp lamp

yam jam

flag bag

lone bone

cart dart

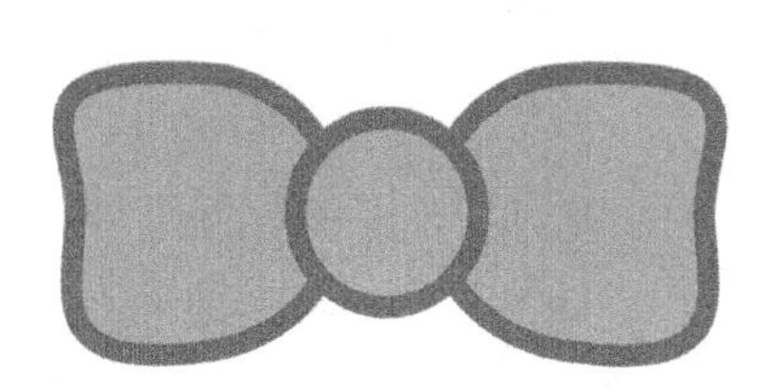

low bow

Name..................................

Read, Circle and Write

light night

mop crop

tap nap

hat pat

sad bad

tin pin

wind fin

drop shop

rib bib

Name......................................

Missing Vowel Sounds

a e i o u

y____k

a e i o u

v____n

a e i o u

t____n

a e i o u

c____w

a e i o u

b____ll

a e i o u

b____ck

a e i o u

b____d

a e i o u

z____p

a e i o u

t____b

Name.................................

Missing Vowel Sounds

a e i o u

b___t

a e i o u

b___g

a e i o u

b___ll

a e i o u

b___x

a e i o u

b___n

a e i o u

b___y

a e i o u

c___r

a e i o u

c___at

a e i o u

sh___ll

Name.......................................

Missing Vowel Sounds

a e i o u

p___t

a e i o u

b___x

a e i o u

d___b

a e i o u

d___y

a e i o u

d___ish

a e i o u

d___d

a e i o u

gr___ss

a e i o u

g___m

a e i o u

h___m

Name................................

Missing Vowel Sounds

a e i o u

h___nd

a e i o u

h___ll

a e i o u

j___r

a e i o u

j___t

a e i o u

k___ng

a e i o u

b___n

a e i o u

m___t

a e i o u

m___n

a e i o u

m___lk

Name.................................

Missing Vowel Sounds

a e i o u

m___m

a e i o u

n___ck

a e i o u

t___g

a e i o u

n___st

a e i o u

n___t

a e i o u

n___se

a e i o u

n___t

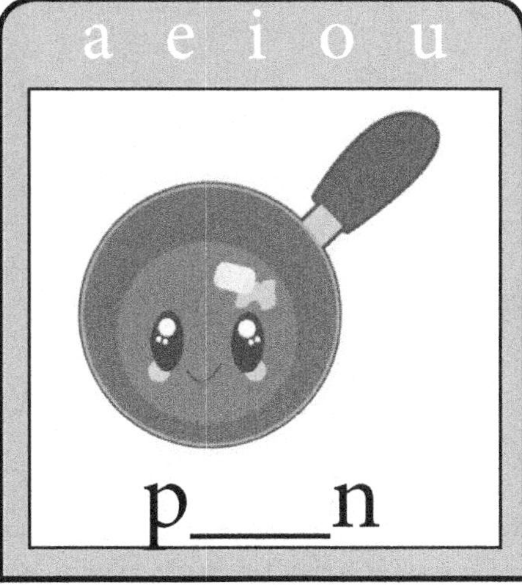

a e i o u

p___n

a e i o u

p___g

Name.................................

Missing Vowel Sounds

Name...............................

Missing Vowel Sounds

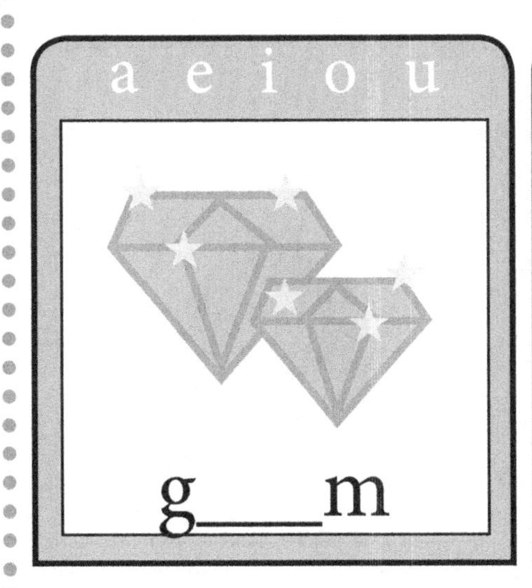

Name..................................

Missing Vowel Sounds

Name...................................

Missing Vowel Sounds

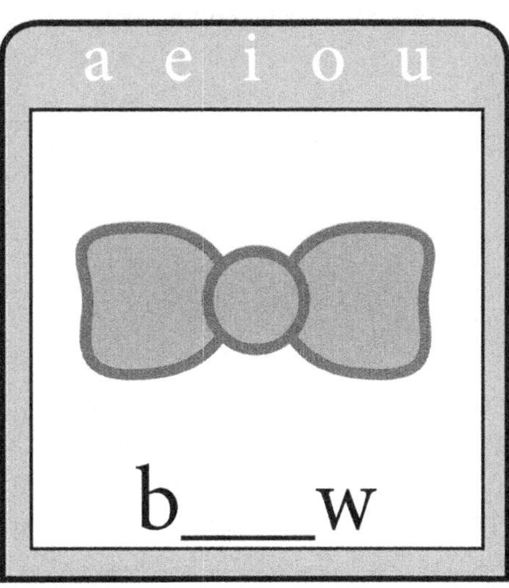

Name.................................

Missing Vowel Sounds

a e i o u

c____rd

a e i o u

l____mp

a e i o u

cl____p

a e i o u

h____t

a e i o u

j____m

a e i o u

c____rt

a e i o u

sh____p

a e i o u

p____n

a e i o u

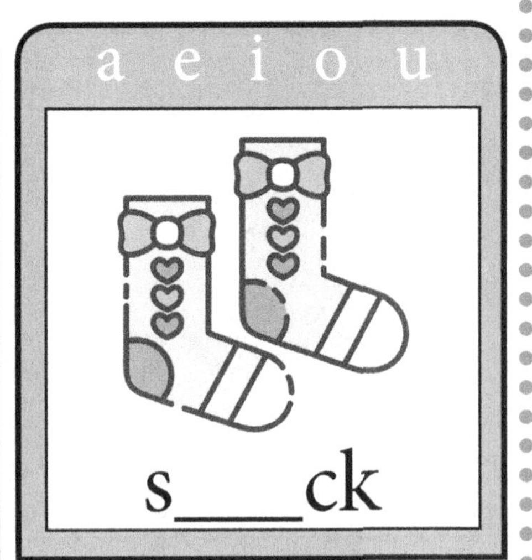

s____ck

Name.......................................

CVC Words Flashcards

Short a - ab	Short a - ab	Short a - ab
cab	dab	gab

Short a - ab	Short a - ab	Short a - ab
jab	lab	nab

Short a - ab	Short a - ab	Short a - ab
tab	crab	grab

Name.................................

CVC Words Flashcards

Short a - at	Short a - at	Short a - at
bat	cat	fat
Short a - at	**Short a - at**	**Short a - at**
hat	mat	pat
Short a - at	**Short a - at**	**Short a - at**
rat	sat	vat

Name.................................

CVC Words Flashcards

Short a - ad	Short a - ad	Short a - ad
bad	dad	had
Short a - ad	Short a - ad	Short a - ad
lad	mad	pad
Short a - ad	Short a - ad	Short a - ad
sad	tad	glad

Name..................................

CVC Words Flashcards

Short a - an	Short a - an	Short a - an
ban	can	fan
Short a - an	Short a - an	Short a - an
man	pan	ran
Short a - an	Short a - an	Short a - an
tan	van	plan

Name.......................................

CVC Words Flashcards

Short a - ag

bag

Short a - ag

gag

Short a - ag

hag

Short a - ag

lag

Short a - ag

nag

Short a - ag

rag

Short a - ag

sag

Short a - ag

tag

Short a - ag

brag

Name..................................

CVC Words Flashcards

Short a - ap	Short a - ap	Short a - ap
cap	gap	lap
Short a - ap	Short a - ap	Short a - ap
map	nap	rap
Short a - ap	Short a - ap	Short a - ap
sap	tap	clap

Name.....................................

CVC Words Flashcards

Short a - am	Short a - am	Short a - am
bam	dam	ham

Short a - am	Short a - am	Short a - am
jam	ram	clam

Short a - am	Short a - am	Short a - am
scam	tram	slam

Name..................................

CVC Words Flashcards

Short a - ack

back

Short a - ack

hack

Short a - ack

jack

Short a - ack

lack

Short a - ack

pack

Short a - ack

rack

Short a - ack

sack

Short a - ack

black

Short a - ack

crack

Name.....................................

CVC Words Flashcards

Short e - ed	Short e - ed	Short e - ed
bed	fed	led

Short e - ed	Short e - ed	Short e - ed
red	wed	bled

Short e - ed	Short e - ed	Short e - ed
bred	shed	sled

Name.................................

CVC Words Flashcards

Short e - et	Short e - et	Short e - et
bet	**get**	**jet**
Short e - et	Short e - et	Short e - et
let	**met**	**net**
Short e - et	Short e - et	Short e - et
pet	**set**	**wet**

Name................................

CVC Words Flashcards

Short e - en	Short e - en	Short e - en
den	hen	men
Short e - en	Short e - en	Short e - en
pen	ten	zen
Short e - en	Short e - en	Short e - en
ben	then	when

Name.................................

CVC Words Flashcards

Short e - ell	Short e - ell	Short e - ell
bell	**cell**	**dell**

Short e - ell	Short e - ell	Short e - ell
jell	**sell**	**tell**

Short e - ell	Short e - ell	Short e - ell
well	**yell**	**shell**

Name..................................

CVC Words Flashcards

Short i - it	Short i - it	Short i - it
bit	fit	hit
Short i - it	Short i - it	Short i - it
kit	lit	pit
Short i - it	Short i - it	Short i - it
sit	knit	quit

Name..................................

CVC Words Flashcards

Short i - id	Short i - id	Short i - id
bid	did	hid

Short i - id	Short i - id	Short i - id
kid	lid	rid

Short i - id	Short i - id	Short i - id
skid	slid	mid

Name.................................

CVC Words Flashcards

Short i - ig	Short i - ig	Short i - ig
big	dig	fig

Short i - ig	Short i - ig	Short i - ig
gig	jig	pig

Short i - ig	Short i - ig	Short i - ig
rig	wig	zig

Name.....................................

CVC Words Flashcards

Short i - im	Short i - im	Short i - im
dim	him	rim
Short i - im	Short i - im	Short i - im
jim	tim	grim
Short i - im	Short i - im	Short i - im
skim	slim	swim

Name.....................................

CVC Words Flashcards

Short i - ip	Short i - ip	Short i - ip
dip	hip	lip
Short i - ip	Short i - ip	Short i - ip
nip	rip	sip
Short i - ip	Short i - ip	Short i - ip
tip	zip	chip

Name..............................

CVC Words Flashcards

Short i - ip	Short i - ip	Short i - ip
clip	drip	flip

Short i - ip	Short i - ip	Short i - ip
grip	ship	skip

Short i - ip	Short i - ip	Short i - ip
slip	snip	trip

Name..................................

CVC Words Flashcards

Short i - ick	Short i - ick	Short i - ick
kick	lick	nick
Short i - ick	Short i - ick	Short i - ick
pick	sick	tick
Short i - ick	Short i - ick	Short i - ick
wick	brick	chick

Name.......................................

CVC Words Flashcards

Short i - in	Short i - in	Short i - in
bin	din	fin
pin	sin	tin
win	chin	grin

Name....................................

CVC Words Flashcards

Short o - ot	Short o - ot	Short o - ot
cot	dot	got
Short o - ot	Short o - ot	Short o - ot
hot	jot	lot
Short o - ot	Short o - ot	Short o - ot
not	pot	rot

Name......................................

CVC Words Flashcards

Short o - ot	Short o - ot	Short o - ot
tot	blot	knot

Short o - ot	Short o - ot	Short o - ot
plot	shot	slot

Short o - ot	Short o - ot	Short o - ot
spot	snot	clot

Name..............................

CVC Words Flashcards

Short o - ob	Short o - ob	Short o - ob
cob	gob	job
Short o - ob	Short o - ob	Short o - ob
lob	mob	rob
Short o - ob	Short o - ob	Short o - ob
sob	blob	glob

Name.......................................

CVC Words Flashcards

Short o - og	Short o - og	Short o - og
bog	**cog**	**dog**

Short o - og	Short o - og	Short o - og
fog	**hog**	**jog**

Short o - og	Short o - og	Short o - og
log	**blog**	**frog**

Name.......................................

CVC Words Flashcards

Short o - op	Short o - op	Short o - op
cop	hop	mop
Short o - op	Short o - op	Short o - op
pop	top	chop
Short o - op	Short o - op	Short o - op
crop	drop	flop

Name.....................................

CVC Words Flashcards

Short o - ock	Short o - ock	Short o - ock
dock	lock	rock

Short o - ock	Short o - ock	Short o - ock
sock	tock	block

Short o - ock	Short o - ock	Short o - ock
clock	flock	rock

Name................................

CVC Words Flashcards

Short u - ut	Short u - ut	Short u - ut
but	cut	gut
Short u - ut	Short u - ut	Short u - ut
hut	jut	nut
Short u - ut	Short u - ut	Short u - ut
rut	shut	smut

Name.....................................

CVC Words Flashcards

Short u - ub	Short u - ub	Short u - ub
cub	hub	nub
Short u - ub	Short u - ub	Short u - ub
rub	sub	tub
Short u - ub	Short u - ub	Short u - ub
grub	snub	stub

Name.....................................

CVC Words Flashcards

Short u - ug	Short u - ug	Short u - ug
bug	dug	hug
Short u - ug	Short u - ug	Short u - ug
jug	lug	mug
Short u - ug	Short u - ug	Short u - ug
pug	rug	tug

Name..................................

CVC Words Flashcards

Short u - um	Short u - um	Short u - um
bum	gum	hum

Short u - um	Short u - um	Short u - um
mum	sum	chum

Short u - um	Short u - um	Short u - um
drum	glum	plum

Name.................................

CVC Words Flashcards

Short u - un	Short u - un	Short u - un
bun	fun	gun

Short u - un	Short u - un	Short u - un
nun	pun	run

Short u - un	Short u - un	Short u - un
sun	spun	stun

Name................................

CVC Words Flashcards

Short u - ud	Short u - ud	Short u - ud
bud	cud	dud
mud	spud	stud
thud	scud	crud

Name.....................................

CVC Words Flashcards

Short u - uck	Short u - uck	Short u - uck
buck	duck	luck
Short u - uck	Short u - uck	Short u - uck
muck	puck	suck
Short u - uck	Short u - uck	Short u - uck
tuck	yuck	truck

Name.................................

CVC Words Flashcards

Short u - ush	Short u - ush	Short u - ush
gush	hush	lush
Short u - ush	Short u - ush	Short u - ush
mush	rush	blush
Short u - ush	Short u - ush	Short u - ush
brush	crush	flush

Made in the USA
Coppell, TX
11 September 2023